So You Think You Know About...

TYRANNOSAURUS
REX?

BEN GARROD

So You Think You Know About...
TYRANNOSAURUS REX?

Kane Miller
A DIVISION OF EDC PUBLISHING

First American Edition 2019
Kane Miller, A Division of EDC Publishing

First published in the UK in 2018 by Zephyr, an imprint of Head of Zeus, Ltd
Text © Ben Garrod, 2018
Paleo Art © Scott Hartman, 2018, and Gabriel Ugueto, 2018
Cartoon illustrations © Ethan Kocak, 2018
Designed by Sue Michniewicz

The moral right of Ben Garrod to be identified as the author and of
Scott Hartman, Gabriel Ugueto and Ethan Kocak to be identified as the
artists of this work have been asserted.

For information contact:
Kane Miller, A Division of EDC Publishing
PO Box 470663
Tulsa, OK 74147-0663
www.kanemiller.com
www.usbornebooksandmore.com
www.edcpub.com

Library of Congress Control Number: 2018958281

Printed and bound in the United States of America
2 3 4 5 6 7 8 9 10
ISBN: 978-1-61067-857-5

For all those kids who are proud
to be geeky

CONTENTS

Dr. "Boneboy" Ben is a very special geek indeed. Not a week goes by when I don't get on the phone to ask Dr. Ben a question about obscure, strange aspects of biology, and he always has the answers. The reader of this book is very lucky to have such a terrific teacher!

The study of science makes sense of everything in our world. Science makes everything work, and the genius scientists behind technology genuinely are the most powerful people in the world . . .

INTRODUCTION
by **Steve Backshall**

Paleontology, or dino science, is not just about unearthing old stone bones, it's about understanding our planet, and everything that has ever lived on it. By bringing it to life for a new generation, Dr. Ben is connecting you to our past, and making you a part of the knowledge of our future. As he says, there is nothing wrong with being clever; you should embrace your inner geek, and see the world as a puzzle waiting to be solved . . .

Enjoy the adventure.

Hey, Guys

Imagine if there was something that each and every one of us had access to, every single day. Something **fun**, **fascinating** and **free**. Something that can show you some of the most amazing things on (and off) our planet. Sounds too good to be true, doesn't it?

Well, that amazing thing is **science**.

Science is all around us and controls everything – from the sunrise and birds singing to making a milkshake, and even how a dinosaur fossil is formed. If you're interested in science then you can go on the most **exciting adventure** in the galaxy.

If you're thinking "what a geek," you're right, but I think we all should be geeks and take pride in it. Being a geek just means you're really passionate about a topic. I'm geeky about the natural world and always have been.

When I was at school doing cross-country, I found the body of a six-foot shark on the beach and ran back to school with it over my shoulder to dissect at lunchtime. My PE teacher was not impressed.

I'm very geeky about bones. I've studied them, teach about them and I have a collection in my home (with the necessary permits, of course). My skeleton monkey, Lola, is in my living room, lying on a branch above my sofa. Being geeky gives you the **inspiration** and **drive** you need to push forward and achieve whatever you want.

I've worked with **walruses** and **polar bears** in Svalbard, studied **sharks** in Madagascar and even lived with a group of wild **chimpanzees** in an African forest.

Now, I'm an evolutionary biologist and I study any animal that changes over time.

I've been **fascinated** with fossils and dinosaurs since I saw my first fossil when I was five years old on a beach in Norfolk, UK. My dad found a little rock, about as long as my finger. One end was blunt and the other end was pointed. The center was hollow. It looked like a stone bullet to me, and my dad said that was what it was: a belemnite bullet . . . the fossilized shell of a **prehistoric** squid, from more than **100 million years ago.** The world must have looked so different when the dinosaurs were around, and it started me thinking about dinosaurs and other prehistoric animals – how they lived, what they looked like and how they behaved. What did a *Stegosaurus* **eat** for breakfast? How **fast** was a *Tyrannosaurus rex*? How big were *Brontosaurus* **poops**? I had so many questions.

So You Think You Know About . . . Dinosaurs? looks at the most well-known dinosaur species (and a few of the random, weird ones) and uses some of the most modern and interesting science to reveal how your favorite dinosaurs ate enough food every day to fill a dumpster, how they hunted in the dark and why some predators became vegetarians. **Amazing discoveries** will show what dinosaurs looked like, what color they were and even what sounds they made. These books include lots of brand-new science, bringing you the latest discoveries from around the world.

Let's get geeky!

Ben

CHAPTER 1

Dinosaur Definitions

WHAT *IS* A DINOSAUR?

Let's start with something easy.
We should look at **what a dinosaur is**.

What actually IS a dinosaur? It's one of those big, scary lizard things, isn't it?

What, like a *Tyrannosaurus rex*?

Yeah. What about crocodiles? Are they dinosaurs?

No, not crocodiles. They're different.

So, dinosaurs are just big, extinct reptiles?

Well, sort of yes and sort of no. Dinosaurs are technically included in the reptile group, but not really in the way we see reptiles today. And not all dinosaurs are extinct.

What? Dinosaurs are all dead.

No, birds are living dinosaurs, according to the way science groups related species.

So a chicken is a dinosaur?

Yep.

And ostriches?

Yep.

Even cute little garden birds?

Yes – all birds!

But not crocodiles?

No – no reptiles. So, no pliosaurs. No dimetrodons. No pterosaurs.

Wow, so what IS a dinosaur? Am I a dinosaur???

It's complicated. And no, you're not a dinosaur.

There are lots of things we think might be dinosaurs and some things that many of us think definitely can't be dinosaurs, but we don't have a definition that we all agree on. Yes, that's right, there's no universal definition of "dinosaur." Unbelievable, right?

So why not? Basically dinosaurs were everywhere and they all looked different. Next time you're shopping, look in the fruit and vegetable section and try to separate them in your mind. Which are fruits? And which are vegetables? Tomatoes are fruits and yet we don't have them in fruit salad. See what I mean? Then there are the nuts. And peanuts aren't even nuts! It gets really complicated really quickly. And dinosaurs are a lot more confusing than a trip to the supermarket.

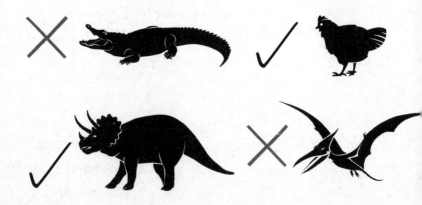

Let's start at the beginning with the word itself. "Dinosaurs" as a group were introduced to the scientific world in 1842 by famous paleontologist Sir Richard Owen (the guy who created the London Natural History Museum). The "dino-" part of the word comes from the Greek for *"terrible"* and "-saur" (or "saurus") from the Greek for *"lizard."* So, *"terrible lizard"* . . . not because they had terrifying claws and teeth, but because Richard Owen wanted to give them a name that showed they were big, awesome and cool. And by the way, they're not actually lizards. They're part of the reptile family, but out on the edge – they're like the funny cousins of the reptiles. We all have weird cousins, right? They're part of the same family as us (but only *just* and they look and behave very differently).

So, dinosaurs weren't terrible and they weren't lizards. We still need to find a way of knowing what a dinosaur is and what it is not. As with the fruit and vegetables in your supermarket, there were a lot of different sizes and shapes of dinosaurs. Some were carnivores, others were herbivores and some were omnivores. There was everything from fish catchers, meat eaters and insect guzzlers to leaf nibblers and seed munchers. They could fly, swim, run, climb . . . except, not all of them could do all these.

Tyrannosaurus rex certainly **didn't fly**.

 Some dinosaurs were **bipedal** and walked on two legs (like *Allosaurus*).

Some were **quadrupedal** and walked on four legs (like *Stegosaurus*).

 Some could happily walk on **two** or **four** legs (like *Iguanodon*), depending on their mood.

Some dinosaurs were **tiny** and could sit on your shoulder (and still probably bite your ear off).

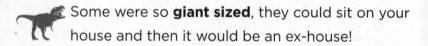 Some were so **giant sized**, they could sit on your house and then it would be an ex-house!

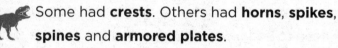 Some had **crests**. Others had **horns**, **spikes**, **spines** and **armored plates**.

So far, around **1,000 different species** of dinosaurs have been identified. This number will get bigger as scientists find more and more fossils and use more high-tech equipment to look at the fossils that are already in museums and universities.

DEFINITELY DINOSAURS

With that many species and so many looking so different, we have to be careful about deciding if a fossil is a dinosaur or not. We base the decision on just a few features of a fossil. Here are three things all dinosaurs have in common:

1. Dinosaurs have two holes behind each eye toward the back of the skull. This means they are diapsids.

If you're wondering, we (as mammals) belong to the synapsid group, all of which have only one hole behind each eye. When you're in your local museum, look at any dinosaur skeleton. The skull should have two holes just behind the eye.

2. Dinosaurs all had straight legs. Next time you see a crocodile when you're out for a walk, have a look at its legs (just don't get too close). Rather than legs that stand straight like ours, their legs bend out in the middle somewhere. All reptiles with legs, such as crocs and their relatives and many lizards, have legs that

CROCODILE

DINOSAUR

21

look the same – they come out from the body to the side and then go down.

All dinosaurs (whether with four legs or two) walked with their legs held in a straight line beneath their body. This meant dinosaurs could breathe easily as they walked or ran – great for chasing other dinosaurs, or running away from them. It also allowed them to become much bigger than if they had legs with a bend in the middle.

3. Dinosaurs had short arms. We all know that *Tyrannosaurus rex* and its relatives had teeny arms, but almost every dinosaur had forelimbs slightly shorter than you might expect. Have a look at your arms – the upper arm bone (humerus) is only a little longer than the two lower arm bones (radius and ulna). In dinosaurs, the radius is nearly always at least 20 percent shorter than the humerus.

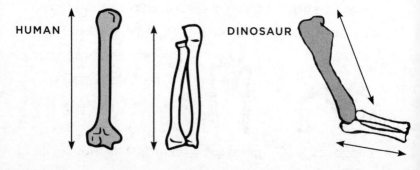

HUMAN   DINOSAUR

DINO CHECKLIST

Between the two holes behind the eye, there is a dimple (called a **fossa**) in the bone.

Most of the neck bones (**vertebrae**) have extra bits of bone that look like a little diagonally backward-facing wing on each side. These are called "**epipophyses**" (*eppi-pofe ee-sees*).

There is a ridge along the edge of the **humerus** for big muscles to attach to. In dinosaurs, this ridge is more than 30 percent of the way along the bone.

The ridge (called the **fourth trochanter**) on the **femur** (thigh bone), which the leg muscles attach to, is strong and looks "sharp."

The bones at the back of the **skull** do not meet in the middle.

The ridge on the **tibia** (shin bone) curves to the front and outward.

At the place where the **fibula** (one of the lower leg bones) joins the ankle, there's a dip on the ankle bone.

There are a lot of other things on the scientists' dino checklist they use to see if they have found a dinosaur fossil. If we can check them *all* off, we can be 100 percent sure it's a dinosaur.

Some of these things are obvious on some fossils and almost impossible to see on others. To spot all of them, you will have to *really* know what to look for. Have a good look at a dinosaur fossil next time you're at your local museum.

CHAPTER 2

Dinosaur Detectives

Tyrannosaurus rex

It's probably *the* most famous dinosaur and one of the best-known animals ever. Everyone knows the *Tyrannosaurus rex*, right? This dinosaur is one of the coolest predators in history. Even the name gives it a big, scary reputation. "*Tyrannos*" comes from the Greek for *tyrant* (another word for a super bully), "*saurus*" we already know means *lizard*, and "*rex*" means *king* in Latin – so, it basically means "*tyrant lizard king*."

Tyrannosaurus rex was one of the largest theropods (two-legged predatory dinosaurs such as *Allosaurus*, *Giganotosaurus* and *Carnotaurus*) and it lived in what is now the western part of North America.

The first bits of a *Tyrannosaurus rex* to be discovered were a handful of teeth found in 1874 in Colorado by Arthur Lakes, a geologist and artist. Bits of bone were found a few years later and, in 1900, a curator (whose nickname was "Mr. Bones") from the American Museum of Natural History found the first semi-complete skeleton of this exciting new species.

But it wasn't always called *Tyrannosaurus rex* – its original name was *Dynamosaurus imperiosus*. The name *Tyrannosaurus rex* was first used in 1906, and when scientists realized they had given one species two different names, they decided to go with *Tyrannosaurus rex*.

The largest, most complete *Tyrannosaurus rex* skeleton was found in 1990, by an amateur paleontologist called Sue Hendrickson. More than 85 percent of the skeleton was found and it's now in the Field Museum of Natural History in Chicago. They bought it for more than $7.5 million – as well as the biggest and most complete *Tyrannosaurus rex*, it is also the most expensive dinosaur skeleton ever. It took over 25,000 hours (that's nearly three years!) to clean the fossil bones to make it look as cool as possible. This skeleton was also from the oldest *Tyrannosaurus rex* we know of and, looking at the bones, scientists think the animal was 28 years old. It looks as though it maybe died from starvation, after eating bad meat and getting sick from the parasites. This amazing fossil is called "Sue," after the woman who discovered it. Imagine having a *Tyrannosaurus rex* fossil named after you!

FAMILY TREE

If I wanted to know everything about you, I could ask you a load of questions, or I could ask your parents or cousins or grandparents. I'd probably find out a lot more that way because they would know extra things about you.

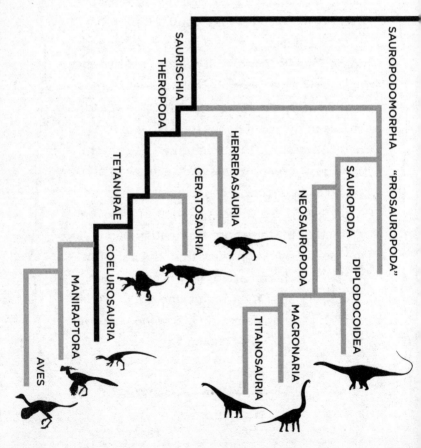

The same is true in nature. If you want to learn all there is to know about a single species, then it helps to look at the other species that are closely related to it. So, what does the *Tyrannosaurus rex* family tree look like?

DINOSAURIA

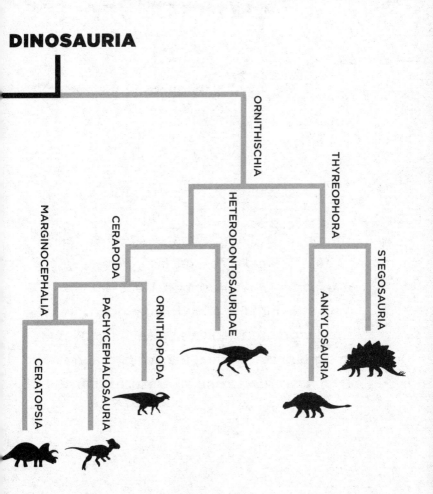

Tyrannosauridae   **Albertosaurinae**

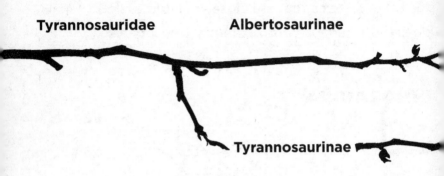

Tyrannosaurinae

Theropods included *Tyrannosaurus rex* (and its cousins) and dinosaurs like *Spinosaurus*, *Allosaurus*, *Giganotosaurus*, *Velociraptor* (and even birds). Within the theropods was a smaller group called Coelurosauria and it's in this group that we find the Tyrannosauridae – *Tyrannosaurus rex* and all its close relatives.

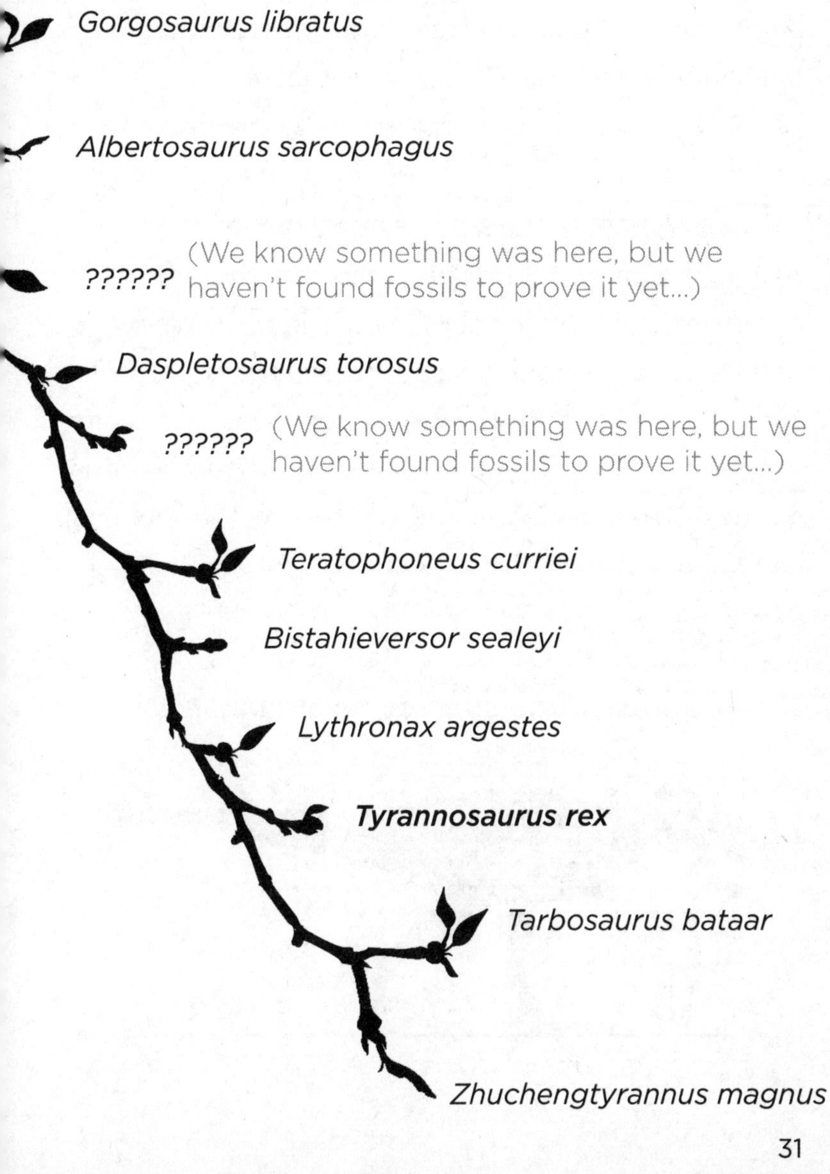

Gorgosaurus libratus

Albertosaurus sarcophagus

?????? (We know something was here, but we haven't found fossils to prove it yet...)

Daspletosaurus torosus

?????? (We know something was here, but we haven't found fossils to prove it yet...)

Teratophoneus curriei

Bistahieversor sealeyi

Lythronax argestes

Tyrannosaurus rex

Tarbosaurus bataar

Zhuchengtyrannus magnus

The tyrannosaurids have two parts to their family – the Albertosaurs and the Tyrannosaurs. Many scientists think there may have been about 11 different branches on the Tyrannosauridae tree, but some think there might only have been three. The truth is that we don't know yet. *Tyrannosaurus rex* was just one single branch.

TYRANNOSAURUS REX RELATIVES

All of the tyrannosaurids were big, two-legged carnivores, with huge skulls and large teeth. They had long legs and were fast for their size, but their arms were small and they usually only had two digits (fingers). Fossils of tyrannosaurids have been found in North America and Asia and when alive, these animals were nearly always the largest predators in their ecosystems.

Tarbosaurus (*Tarbo sore-us*) "alarming lizard"

6 ft.

40 ft.

This tyrannosaurid lived in Asia about 70 million years ago (Late Cretaceous) and fossils have been found in Mongolia and China. Some people believe *Tarbosaurus* is the Asian "cousin" of *Tyrannosaurus* and does not belong to a separate group, but mostly scientists think they were closely related but still different enough.

Although *Tarbosaurus* was smaller than *T. rex*, it could reach up to 40 ft. long and weigh as much as 5 tons (the same as a really big African elephant). It had the smallest arms (compared to body size) of all tyrannosaurids and some special adaptations in its skull.

Albertosaurus (*Albert-o sore-us*) "Alberta lizard"

6 ft.

30 ft.

This predator lived in what is now Canada about 70 million years ago (Late Cretaceous). It was much smaller than its famous relative, *T. rex*.

It could be up to 30 ft. long and weigh about 2 tons (the same as a family car).

Many believe *Albertosaurus* was a pack hunter because fossils from 26 animals were found at just one site, called the "Dry Island bonebed." Scientists discovered an old animal and six young animals, aged between two and 11 years. Maybe they were all scavenging at one carcass, but it could be that they hunted and lived in large groups of mixed ages.

Daspletosaurus (*Daz-pletto sore-us*) "frightful lizard"

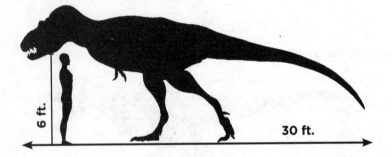

6 ft.

30 ft.

This medium-sized tyrannosaurid lived between 77 and 74 million years ago, in what is now North America.

Daspletosaurus was up to 30 ft. long and could weigh almost 4 tons. It had the longest forelimbs of any tyrannosaurid.

Gorgosaurus (*Gorgo sore-us*) "dreadful lizard"

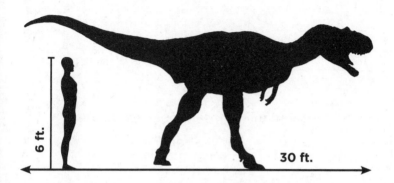

6 ft. 30 ft.

This medium-sized theropod lived about 75 million years ago (Late Cretaceous) in what is now North America. It was closely related to *Albertosaurus*. Because lots of specimens have been found, there are more fossils of *Gorgosaurus* than any other tyrannosaurid.

Gorgosaurus was up to 30 ft. long and weighed around 2-3 tons. It lived in the same areas as *Daspletosaurus* and scientists think the two tyrannosaurids behaved differently and hunted different things, so that they did not fight with each other. *Gorgosaurus* may have hunted hadrosaurs while the bigger, rarer *Daspletosaurus* hunted horned dinosaurs such as *Coronosaurus*.

So You Think You Know About Dinosaurs?

Are all the dinosaurs dead?

•

What does bipedal mean?

•

How many dinosaur species do we know about?

•

What three things do most dinosaurs have in common?

•

What group does *T. rex* belong to?

•

Name two of *T. rex's* relatives.

All the answers are in the text and at the back of the book.

CHAPTER 3

Dinosaur Discoveries

WHEN AND WHERE

WHEN AND WHERE

Tyrannosaurus rex lived in a very small area of the planet and, to be honest, it was one of the last species at the dinosaur party. As a group, dinosaurs existed for about 180 million years before the famous asteroid wiped out all the non-bird dinosaurs. Remember, birds are still dinosaurs. All the dinosaurs lived in the Mesozoic Era.

The Mesozoic Era can be split into three main chunks (what we call "periods") and these are the **Triassic period**, the **Jurassic period** and the **Cretaceous period**. *Tyrannosaurus rex* lived at the very end of the Cretaceous.

Tyrannosaurus rex fossils are found in one particular strip of rock formations at the very end of the Cretaceous period. This strip of time is called the Maastrichtian (*Maz trick-sh-an*) and lasted for just over six million years (72.1–66 million years ago). *Tyrannosaurus rex* fossils are found from between 68–66 million years ago.

The third (and last) period of the dinosaurs, the Cretaceous period, lasted for 79 million years, from 145 million years ago to 66 million years ago. Overall, the climate was fairly warm, with higher sea levels and lots of shallow seas.

On land, dinosaurs still dominated Earth. Although this was the last part of the "Age of Dinosaurs," lots of new groups appeared during this time, such as *Triceratops* and its horned relatives, as well as other famous species, including *Tyrannosaurus rex.*

Before the Cretaceous period, during the Jurassic, flowering plants first evolved. This allowed lots of other species to evolve. Some new dinosaur species would have eaten the plants and others would have eaten the insects that fed on them.

One reason for so many dinosaur species during this time was because of competition between predators and prey, both trying to evolve more quickly than the other. This evolutionary "arms race" meant that predatory species evolved larger teeth and a greater bite force, while prey species evolved horns and spikes to make it more difficult for predators. If a predator evolved to run very quickly over short distances, then maybe a prey species could evolve better vision and the ability to run for longer distances, meaning that they could spot possible predators and outrun them.

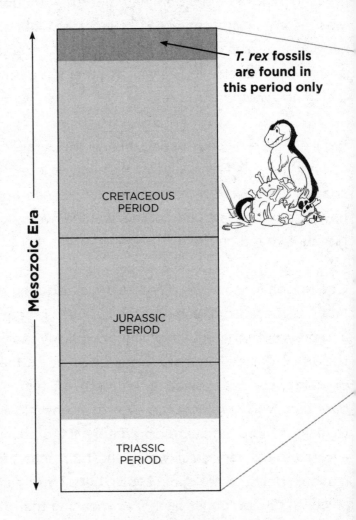

Mesozoic Era

T. rex fossils are found in this period only

CRETACEOUS PERIOD

JURASSIC PERIOD

TRIASSIC PERIOD

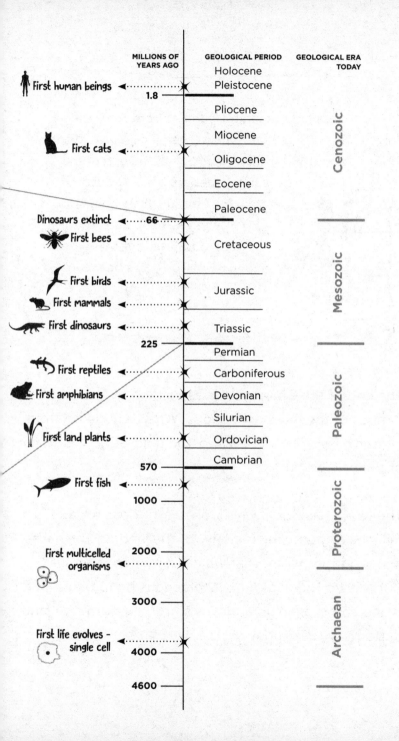

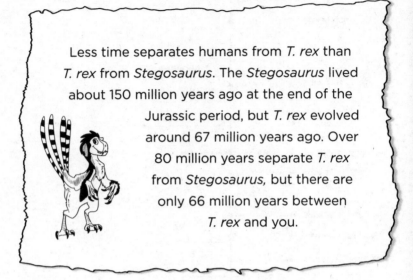

Less time separates humans from *T. rex* than *T. rex* from *Stegosaurus*. The *Stegosaurus* lived about 150 million years ago at the end of the Jurassic period, but *T. rex* evolved around 67 million years ago. Over 80 million years separate *T. rex* from *Stegosaurus,* but there are only 66 million years between *T. rex* and you.

The end of the Cretaceous was marked by the most famous of the mass extinctions. When a huge asteroid hit Earth 66 million years ago, the dinosaurs (well, most of them) died out.

The world has not always looked as it does today. For millions of years, the majority of the land on Earth was lumped together in what we call a "supercontinent." But toward the end of the Cretaceous period, this mega island had broken up and was starting to form the land patterns we see today.

THE WORLD IN THE LATE CRETACEOUS PERIOD:

Laramidia

Tyrannosaurus rex lived throughout what is now western North America, on what was then an island continent known as Laramidia.

The island stretched from what is now Alaska to Mexico, which gave *Tyrannosaurus rex* a wider range than any other tyrannosaurid. It is an area very rich in fossils. Everything from tyrannosaurs and troodons to pachycephalosaurs and titanosaurs have been found here.

On Laramidia, the top predators were the Tyrannosauridae theropods, such as *Tyrannosaurus rex*, *Daspletosaurus*, *Albertosaurus* and *Gorgosaurus*. Although they were all tyrannosaurids, they were not all around at the same time. Laramidia also had a huge number of different types of the duck-billed hadrosaurs.

How fast could *Tyrannosaurus rex* run?

**So many people work with dinosaurs –
from amateur collectors to world-famous scientists.
Some go looking for fossils in the ground, others study
them in laboratories and some recreate them
as incredible pieces of artwork.**

PROFESSOR JOHN HUTCHINSON

Evolutionary biologist

The Royal Veterinary College, London (UK)

Professor John Hutchinson works at The Royal
Veterinary College and specializes in studying what's
called biomechanics — looking at things like how
strong different animals are and how animals move.
He looks at animals alive now, like elephants and
crocodiles, and at extinct animals too. We asked
John how fast a *Tyrannosaurus rex* could run and
how we could find that out.

Tyrannosaurus weighed as much as a really huge elephant and yet supported all that weight on two legs, not four. How did it do that? Could it just walk or could it have run, and if so, how fast? Some paleontologists had argued that it could run as fast as a racehorse (about 40 mph). I wanted to use science to test that. And it was fun!

I developed a new approach by studying how living animals move. I ran emus around my lab, I had crocodiles galloping around a zoo in Florida, and I got to work with over 100 different elephants around the world. How cool is that? I put little sticky markers on their legs so my computer could track how their legs moved, and then I used video cameras to get film of those movements for my computer.

This told me how hard the leg muscles of these living animals had to work to support and move them. Bigger animals like elephants have to use even bigger muscles for their size to run at all. Smaller animals can jump and bounce around and do all kinds of activities that would cause bigger animals to fall apart if they tried.

So, having learned this, I built a computer version of *Tyrannosaurus rex* and asked the computer to tell me how hard its leg muscles would have needed to work for it to run like a racehorse. The computer said, "nope." It couldn't find a way that *Tyrannosaurus rex* could run that fast. Instead, I found out that *Tyrannosaurus rex* might have walked quickly or run as fast as an athletic human (maybe 20 mph at most).

That's not bad, either! Its prey items, like duckbill dinosaurs and *Triceratops*, were also clunky beasts that probably weren't much, or any, faster. Medium-sized, long-legged, muscular dinosaurs such as *Struthiomimus* were probably the fastest.

So when you picture the giant dinosaurs of the Mesozoic Era, don't picture them as racehorses or cheetahs, but as slower but still frightening and impressive animals, like elephants or rhinoceroses. We'll never have to race a *Tyrannosaurus rex*, and that's a very good thing, but the races in the Late Cretaceous period were at a slower pace. Science is our time machine that helps us understand how extinct animals may have worked. Hooray for science!

CHAPTER 4

Delve into a Dinosaur

ANATOMY OF *TYRANNOSAURUS REX*

THE BONES

A *Tyrannosaurus rex* skeleton is not so much sharp and sleek but more about big and extreme power. It's not so much a fast race car – more of a deadly monster truck. The huge skull was wide and powerful and the rest of the skeleton helped make *Tyrannosaurus rex* an ultimate prehistoric predator. Let's have a good look at the skull and then at the rest of the skeleton.

THE SKULL

Some theropods like *Allosaurus* had narrow skulls with sharp, flat teeth for slashing their prey, but *Tyrannosaurus rex* had a huge wide skull with broad teeth.

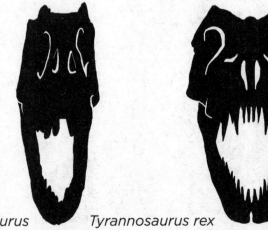

Allosaurus   *Tyrannosaurus rex*

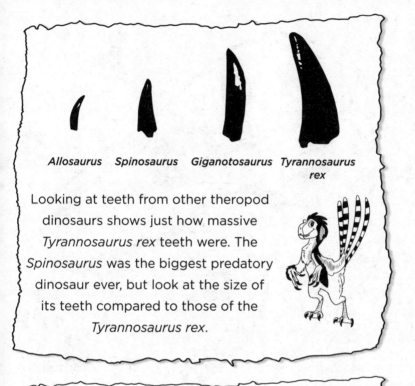

Allosaurus   **Spinosaurus**   **Giganotosaurus**   **Tyrannosaurus rex**

Looking at teeth from other theropod dinosaurs shows just how massive *Tyrannosaurus rex* teeth were. The *Spinosaurus* was the biggest predatory dinosaur ever, but look at the size of its teeth compared to those of the *Tyrannosaurus rex*.

The *Tyrannosaurus rex* had a huge bite force of at least 13,000 PSI (pounds per square inch), but it's hard to imagine just how hard they could bite other beasties. As a puny human, your bite force is just 150 PSI. A great white shark's bite is only about 650 PSI and the saltwater crocodile has the largest bite of any living animal – 3,700 PSI – but *T. rex* still had a bite more than three times stronger. **Ouch!**

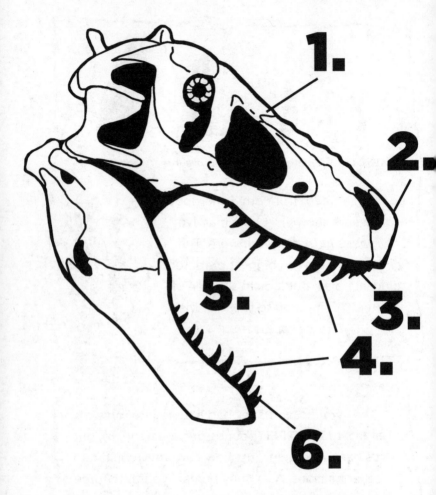

1. Most of the bones in a *Tyrannosaurus rex* skull were **huge** and some were **fused or joined together** to stop them moving about when they were eating. This also helped strengthen the skull and gave *Tyrannosaurus rex* **the most powerful dinosaur bite**.

2. The tip of the upper jaw was D-shaped. This was good and bad. It meant a *Tyrannosaurus rex* could **rip off more flesh with a single bite,** but it also meant more force in the teeth, risking breaks. Most theropods had V-shaped upper jaws.

3. The eight teeth at the tip of the upper jaw were close together and much smaller than the rest. They were D-shaped in cross section and had ridges on the back that made them stronger. They **curved backward** and **had sharp tips**.

4. Unlike most theropods, *Tyrannosaurus rex* was a heterodont, with **different-shaped teeth** in different parts of the mouth.

5. Its cheek teeth were bigger than the teeth at the upper jaw and **good at taking lots of force** when they bit down on **wriggling prey**. These teeth looked like big, fat sharp bananas, not like thin knives.

6. The teeth were used to **hold on to prey** and to **strip its flesh**. The biggest *Tyrannosaurus rex* tooth found so far is about 12 in., making them the largest teeth of any carnivorous dinosaur.

The biggest *T. rex* skulls could reach 5 ft. long.

That's pretty big – much bigger than me!

Measure how tall you are and see if you are bigger than a *T. rex* skull.

THE SKELETON

How did early paleontologists imagine an animal that no human had ever seen? Sometimes, they got it wrong. They thought that *Tyrannosaurus rex* was too big to have walked on just two legs and that it must have balanced on its tail, a bit like a kangaroo. So, many *Tyrannosaurus rex* paintings and skeletons in museums show the dinosaur standing with its tail on the ground and its head high up. This was wrong and actually would have made the joints in the tail, legs and hips weak.

The *Tyrannosaurus rex* is like a dinosaur celebrity and has had a few makeovers over the years. Its posture has changed from a tall, "dino tripod," with two legs and a tail on the ground, to a fast, two-legged predator, with the head and tail in a horizontal position. *Tyrannosaurus rex* has also gone from a scaly green killer to a feathered predator. The *Tyrannosaurus rex* we know now is very different than the one we thought existed a few years ago.

2.

The neck made an S-shaped curve and was also short and had lots of strong muscles.

1.

T. rex had a huge, heavy skull and the eyes were forward facing.

8.

The forelimbs (arms) were short but really powerful.

7.

Each forearm ended in two digits (or fingers) and each of these ended in a sharp claw.

3.

To compensate for the immense bulk of the animal, many bones throughout the skeleton were not solid but were air filled.

4.

The tail was heavy and long.

5.

***T. rex* was a bipedal (two-legged) predator, with big, powerful hind limbs.**

6.

***T. rex* had longer and skinnier toes than similar-sized theropod dinosaurs.**

1. *T. rex* had a huge and heavy skull.

The biggest *T. rex* skulls can be as much as 5 ft. in length. See how big that is compared to how tall you are. The eyes were forward facing, allowing *Tyrannosaurus rex* to have excellent 3-D vision, because there was a big overlap between what each eye could see. This would have helped make it a brilliant predator when chasing prey.

2. The neck made an S-shaped curve and was also short and had lots of strong muscles.

This helped support the massive (and very heavy) head.

3. To compensate for the immense bulk of the animal, many bones throughout the skeleton were not solid but were air filled (like hollow but not quite the same).

This reduced the dinosaur's weight without any significant loss of strength.

4. The tail was heavy and long.

It sometimes contained over 40 vertebrae, in order to balance the massive head and body.

The most complete *T. rex* fossil was more than 40 ft. long and when alive, the animal would have weighed somewhere between 9 and 20 tons.

5. *T. rex* was a bipedal (two-legged) predator, with powerful, big hind limbs.

These big legs were some of the longest in relation to body size of any theropod dinosaur.

6. *T. rex* had longer and skinnier toes than similar-sized theropod dinosaurs such as *Allosaurus*, and its foot bones also interlocked.

This helps show that *T. rex* was a fast-moving predator, faster than other big predators like *Allosaurus*.

7. Each forearm ended in two digits (fingers) and each of these ended in a sharp claw.

There was also an extra little bone called a metacarpal (like one of the long ones at the bottom of each of your fingers in your palm). This shows that at some point *Tyrannosaurus rex* used to have three claws, but the third was lost through evolution.

8. The forelimbs (arms) were short but super powerful.

Tyrannosaurus rex forelimbs were made of extra-thick bone. This probably means they could have taken a lot of force – either gripping struggling prey, pushing themselves up from the ground, or fighting with other *Tyrannosaurus rexes*. Their forearm had a limited range, as the shoulder joint only allowed 40 degrees of movement. If you swing your arm around – go on, try it – your shoulder can rotate a full 360 degrees. It might sound as though the *Tyrannosaurus rex* had useless arms, but maybe this restricted movement meant it could hold on tighter to prey without risking injury.

THE BODY

1.

Many dinosaurs had feathers, so it is possible that *Tyrannosaurus rex* had feathers on at least part of its body.

5.

Scientists are looking into dinosaur colors and are making some amazing (and slightly weird) discoveries.

4.

Tyrannosaurus rex had puny-looking arms (although they were still 3 ft. long).

2.

Tyrannosaurus rex was balanced by a long and heavy tail, to stop it falling forward.

3.

Tyrannosaurus rex possibly had feathers along the top of its tail and scales on the bottom.

1. This bit is complicated. **Many dinosaurs had feathers** – a few years ago, this would have sounded like a crazy thing to say, but now we know that many theropods were either partly or fully covered in feathers. Not the sort of feathers we see in garden birds but more like those of cassowaries and kiwis. For *Tyrannosaurus rex*, there's no proof that it did have feathers, but we do know that other tyrannosaurids such as *Dilong* were feathered. Some fossils of big *Tyrannosaurus rex* relatives have been preserved with feathers, so it makes sense that *Tyrannosaurus rex* had feathers on at least part of its body.

2. Because the *Tyrannosaurus rex* walked with its **huge, heavy head low and forward**, it needed to be balanced by a long and heavy tail. **The tail acted like a set of weighing scales** and stopped the *Tyrannosaurus rex* falling forward all the time.

3. Even though we now know that many theropods were feathered and that *Tyrannosaurus rex* was probably at least partly feathered, do we know how much of the body was covered in feathers? We can have a good guess (with the help of some funky fossils). The fossil of a small relative of *Tyrannosaurus rex* called *Juravenator* was found with a feathered body and a tail half covered in feathers (along the top) and half covered in scales (along the bottom). Other less complete tyrannosaurid fossils have been found with similar markings on the tail, so it makes a lot of sense to think that probably (but not definitely), **_Tyrannosaurus rex_ had feathers across a lot of its body and along the top of the tail.**

4. Even though _Tyrannosaurus rex_ had puny-looking arms (they were still 3 ft. long), they were strong. The biceps muscle alone of an adult _Tyrannosaurus rex_ could lift over 400 lb. (more than two adult humans) and with all the muscles combined, _Tyrannosaurus rex_ was probably even stronger than this. Its biceps was over three times more powerful than the same muscle in humans. **Basically, a _Tyrannosaurus rex_ would definitely win if you arm wrestled one.**

5. A lot of people want to know what color dinosaurs were. Were they green or brown, as we often see them depicted in books, or were they blue, yellow or pink, even? Scientists are looking into dinosaur colors and are making some amazing (and slightly weird) discoveries. Check out the "New Science" section starting on page 75 to learn more.

So You Think You Know About Dinosaurs?

How long is the biggest *T. rex* tooth
found so far?

•

Which period did *T. rex* live in?

•

Which period did the first
flowering plants evolve in?

•

What is Laramidia?

•

How many vertebrae in
a *T. rex*'s tail?

*All the answers are in the text
and at the back of the book.*

CHAPTER 5

Dinosaur Domains

HABITATS AND ECOSYSTEMS

HABITATS AND ECOSYSTEMS

We already know that *Tyrannosaurus rex* lived right at the end of the time when dinosaurs dominated life on Earth and only died out 66 million years ago. This

stage is called the Maastrichtian age (at the very end of the Cretaceous period). In the early part of the Late Cretaceous period, the climate was warm. It became cooler at the end of the Late Cretaceous, but Earth

was still warmer than it is today. Tropical areas were near the Equator (the same as now). The far north and south (what are the cold polar regions today) were more temperate and had seasons like ours, with warmer summers and colder winters. This probably meant that some dinosaurs needed to migrate during the year to follow food and warmer conditions. It was still too warm for there to be ice at either the northern or southern poles at the end of the Late Cretaceous.

Tyrannosaurus rex fossils have been discovered at sites from different ecosystems. They've been found far inland in dry, hot plains, and along the coast in areas that were almost tropical. One famous fossil site called Hell Creek, was at the time subtropical, with a humid and warm climate.

It seems as though *Tyrannosaurus rex* lived in different ecosystems, or maybe moved between them, and liked different habitats. Their fossils have been found in forests, with redwoods, magnolias, willows and monkey puzzle

trees all around. Many of these forests were open and close to rivers. Fossils have also been found near the coast and swampy forest.

Maybe these were the best places to find their main food.

By looking at the fossils of their prey, such as *Triceratops* and *Edmontosaurus*, scientists think that *Tyrannosaurus rex* crushed and broke bones as it ate. Broken bones have also been found in its dung. When the *Tyrannosaurus rex* was around, *Triceratops* was one of the most common large herbivores in the northern part of its range. In the southern

part, a sauropod called *Alamosaurus* was common and an important part of the *Tyrannosaurus rex* food chain.

Tyrannosaurus rex shared its northern ecosystem with a range of different species. How many do you know and which ones do you think would have ended up as *Tyrannosaurus rex* lunch?

Tyrannosaurus shared its southern ecosystem with some of the same species found in its northern range, but there was also a different bunch of species down south.

These dinosaurs lived at the same time as *Tyrannosaurus rex*. Which ones do you think *T. rex* would have hunted?

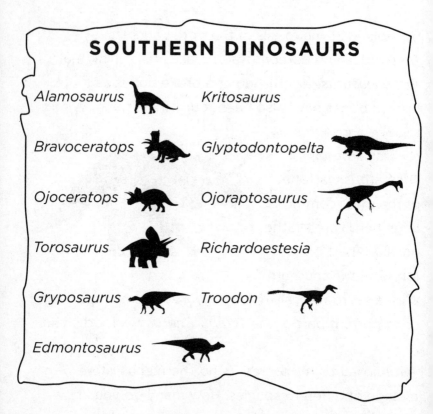

SOUTHERN DINOSAURS

Alamosaurus   *Kritosaurus*

Bravoceratops   *Glyptodontopelta*

Ojoceratops   *Ojoraptosaurus*

Torosaurus   *Richardoestesia*

Gryposaurus   *Troodon*

Edmontosaurus

NORTHERN DINOSAURS

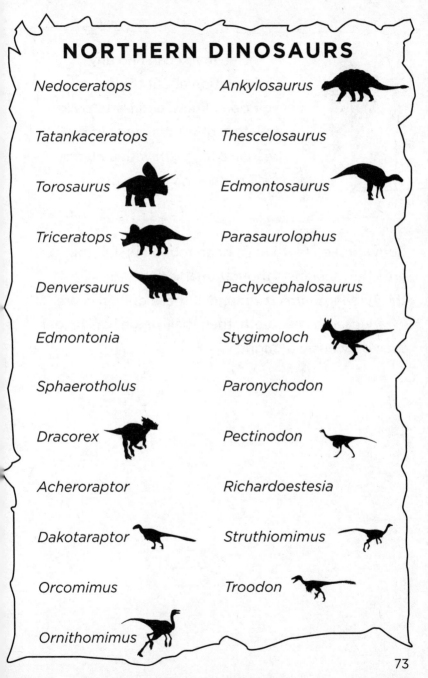

Nedoceratops

Tatankaceratops

Torosaurus

Triceratops

Denversaurus

Edmontonia

Sphaerotholus

Dracorex

Acheroraptor

Dakotaraptor

Orcomimus

Ornithomimus

Ankylosaurus

Thescelosaurus

Edmontosaurus

Parasaurolophus

Pachycephalosaurus

Stygimoloch

Paronychodon

Pectinodon

Richardoestesia

Struthiomimus

Troodon

See if you can find any information about the animals you don't know, and try to build a picture of what life would have been like for them with a hungry *T. rex* always on the prowl.

Some broken teeth have been found outside the area that scientists thought marked the edge of the *Tyrannosaurus rex* range. If these definitely are *Tyrannosaurus rex* teeth, then their range was bigger than previously thought.

Feather Colors

Studying dinosaurs can seem weird. They lived millions of years ago, but we are still learning so much about them. Technology is advancing all the time, allowing us to do more than ever before. We can use scanners to look inside bones without cutting them in half and we can even fire lasers at fossils to reveal details of skin and tendons that we could never see with our eyes or with microscopes. Dinosaurs may be old, but the science of dinosaurs is brand-new and there is "new science" all the time.

We want to know more and more about them. What did they eat? We look at their fossil poop to find out. How fast could they run? Easy, make a fancy computer program and get some emus to help you. What color were they? Ah, well, that's not quite so easy to answer. Fossil skin is rarely preserved and even when it is, the color is impossible to tell. So will we ever know if dinosaurs were green all over or stripy and orange, for example?

A few years ago, a team of scientists had a breakthrough. We now know that many dinosaurs (especially the theropods) had feathers. And we know that feathers in birds today are all different colors. Was there a way to find out what colors the feathers were? Yes, there was. Melanosomes.

Melanosomes are tiny structures (called organelles) that give many things in nature their color and they can be found in feathers and in the hair of mammals. Your hair color is determined by the types of melanosomes within your hair.

These structures code for certain colors – mainly black, gray, orange and brown – but they can also create iridescence (like a shiny or oily effect) and give a bright-blue appearance. Think about birds such as starlings, magpies and jays.

Melanosomes are a vital part of the tough structure of feathers, which, luckily, means that they can survive fossilization and can still be seen millions of years later, if the fossil preservation is good. All scientists had to do was look at fossil feathers, find the melanosomes, match them against the different colored feathers found on birds today and "ta-daaa," they would be able to tell what color feathered dinosaurs were.

This is sort of what the scientists did. By looking at the fossilized feathers under a scanning electron microscope (a very high-powered microscope), they were able to see the organization and shape of melanosomes within the structure of the fossil feathers. Not only that, some fossils showed clear bands across them, so that you didn't need a microscope to see that they would have been stripy when the dinosaur was alive.

UNDER THE MICROSCOPE

You can't actually see the colors on a fossil feather, but if you look under a microscope you can see the tiny melanosomes.

MODERN FEATHER

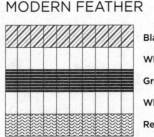

Black
White
Green
White
Red

How they are arranged gives all the different colors we can see on modern feathers. This simple diagram shows how the arrangement gives us the colors. If we look at modern melanosome arrangements, then we can predict what the fossil feathers looked like.

FOSSIL FEATHER

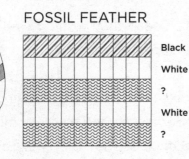

Black
White
?
White
?

Can you use the information from the modern feather to tell what colors the fossil feather was?

This was first achieved on a very small dinosaur called *Sinosauropteryx*. This little theropod was from China and would have lived during the Early Cretaceous. *Sinosauropteryx* had very short arms and a very long tail. In total, it was just over 3 ft. in length and would have weighed approximately 16 oz.

Some *Sinosauropteryx* fossils show rings of darker and lighter bands running along the tail. To start with, some scientists thought this was a problem with how the fossil was preserved, but we now know it was because these bands were different colors when the little dinosaur was alive.

The team also believes that the top side of the body was darker than the underside. When they looked at the melanosomes to see what actual colors *Sinosauropteryx* was, they found a mixture of pale, creamy feathers and darker, orangey feathers. The feathers on the tail of

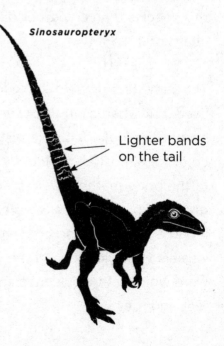

Sinosauropteryx

Lighter bands on the tail

Sinosauropteryx were not like the feathers on birds we see today. Instead, they were simple bristly structures – more proto-feather than actual feather – but that didn't matter. Scientists had discovered what sort of colors dinosaurs were. And the first one was stripy and orange.

Another dinosaur to get the color treatment is the very cool *Anchiornis huxleyi* (literally meaning "Huxley's nearly bird"). Hundreds of *Anchiornis* fossils have been found in China, dating back 160 million years (into the Late Jurassic period). It is said that more is known about this species than any other dinosaur. Have you even heard of it?

The same technique of looking at melanosomes was used, but whereas in *Sinosauropteryx* only parts of the body were looked at, scientists were able to identify the color for almost all of *Anchiornis*. They found that most of the body feathers were black and gray. The face was gray too, but the cheeks were an orange-red color and it had a funky-looking crown on the top of its head that was also orangey red. All the wings (it sort of had four) were white with black ends and edges, and it had black feet and toes.

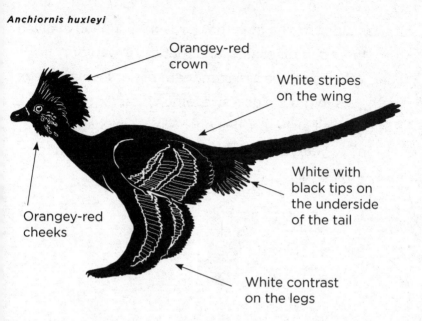

Anchiornis huxleyi

Orangey-red crown

White stripes on the wing

White with black tips on the underside of the tail

Orangey-red cheeks

White contrast on the legs

Learning the color of dinosaurs is important in better understanding the whole group. It allowed scientists to debate the original use of feathers – were they for flight, for keeping warm, or for display? Because the feathers on *Sinosauropteryx* were useless for keeping warm and would not have allowed flight but were still colored, we think that feathers first evolved for display and showing off. Birds often have amazingly colored plumage, used for either camouflage or courtship display, so it makes sense that dinosaurs would have done the same. This discovery has huge benefits to our knowledge of dinosaur ecology and behavior.

It also supports the idea that birds have indeed evolved from theropod dinosaurs, and that the group of adaptations that we see in modern birds, such as wings, feathers, a big brain and awesome visual system and a lightweight skeleton, has been slowly evolving over millions of years through the dinosaurs, finally giving rise to the birds.

CHAPTER 6

Dodging Dinosaurs

EVOLUTIONARY ARMS RACE

EVOLUTIONARY ARMS RACE

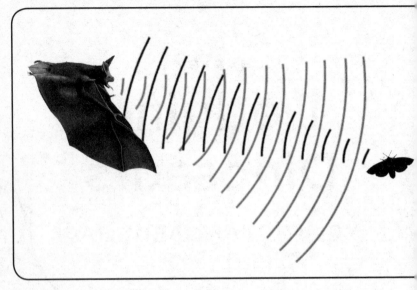

Lots of things drive evolution forward, making a species change over time. It could be the particular habitat (such as a cold environment makes polar bears have very small ears), or feeding techniques (just think about giraffes), but it might be down to competition between predators and prey. The term for this is an evolutionary arms race, where as the predator species evolves in a way to increase its chances of catching and eating the prey, the prey species also evolves to reduce the chances of ending up as lunch. Then the predator evolves to increase its chances again and so does the prey, and so on and so on. It never ends and both species are trying to do what is best for them.

Evolutionary arms races are happening everywhere in nature, but one very cool example is between bats and moths. Bats make high-frequency clicks and squeaks that bounce off flying moths (like echoes) so that the bat can detect them. Most moths then evolved specialized ears that can detect these bat calls, so they can avoid them. Then some bats evolved stealth echolocation so the moths wouldn't hear them.

And some moths then evolved their own special clicks that confuse the bats when they are hunting. So, both are evolving constantly to outdo each other.

I love using examples like this to help us understand dinosaurs. All animals today are battling for survival.

THE BATTLE

Dinosaurs were part of all this and an example of the evolutionary arms race would be between *Tyrannosaurus rex* and *Triceratops*. *Triceratops* was one of the dominant large herbivores around the time *Tyrannosaurus rex* lived and there is no doubt they would have met. They probably wouldn't have been the best of friends, but who would win in a fight? Just because *Tyrannosaurus rex* was a fearsome predator doesn't mean that *Triceratops* was an easy meal.

OK, imagine the scene: a fully grown female *Tyrannosaurus rex* has just walked through the forest and around a pile of rocks near a shallow river. As well as good eyesight and hearing, *Tyrannosaurus rex* had large olfactory lobes, meaning she probably had an excellent sense of smell. She was perfectly adapted for hunting prey.

She spots a single *Triceratops* near the edge of the water and quietly stalks it. The *Tyrannosaurus rex* lowers her massive head and crouches, watching with her forward-facing eyes and judging how far away the prey is with her amazing 3-D vision.

The *Triceratops* is a mature bull male. He's drinking far away from the rest of the herd and is always alert. Eyes on the side of his head allow him to scan the surrounding area for predators or other large male *Triceratops*.

The bull *Triceratops* sees movement near the rocks a short distance away. He lifts his head and turns his body toward the movement, in a defensive position. The *Tyrannosaurus rex* stands up and moves closer. Holding her head low and tail high gives her excellent balance. Despite weighing over 14 tons, she is fast.

She runs over to the *Triceratops* and lunges at his side.

The *Triceratops* swings his massive head and aims his horns toward the *Tyrannosaurus rex*. The two long horns above his eyes are each over 3 ft. long and very sharp. The *Tyrannosaurus rex* can no longer get to the softer part of the *Triceratops*' body because the big frill around his head and the horns are in the way and pose a danger. Even though some scientists argue that the *Triceratops* used their horns for display to other *Triceratops* and the frills were either for display or to help control body temperature, they would still have helped fight off a predator like a *Tyrannosaurus rex*.

The *Tyrannosaurus rex* is the faster dinosaur and tries to strike behind *Triceratops*' head. She gets behind the *Triceratops* and shoves him with her huge, powerful head, trying to tip him over, so she can bite into his belly.

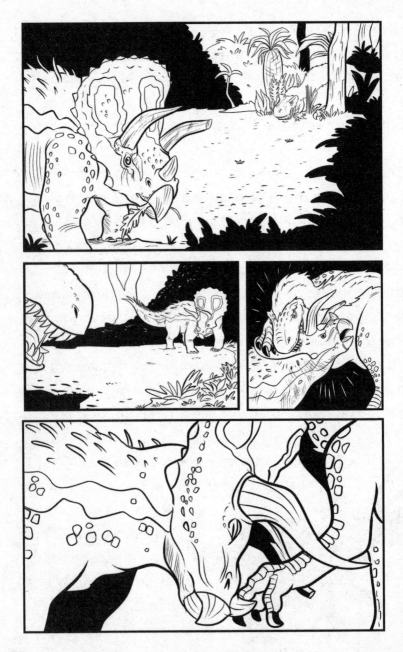

But *Triceratops* were heavy animals and low to the ground. They had what we call a low center of gravity, which meant they could not be knocked over easily. Think about it – if you stand on tiptoe or you crouch down with your feet apart, which makes you easier to knock over? As she knocks into him, he doesn't topple over but instead digs one of his horns into her leg, and she hits the ground. It's very hard to get back up with her small arms, but she manages to stand again and moves back toward him.

She's injured and is slower. She lunges at the *Triceratops* and bites into the edge of his frill. She has the greatest bite force of any dinosaur, over 13,000 PSI – imagine something the weight of a giraffe, standing on less than an inch – and tears a chunk out of the frill, crushing bone and damaging the skull with her teeth. This sounds bad but no organs are affected and the *Triceratops* is not seriously injured. But he is mad. He charges at the *Tyrannosaurus rex* and she backs off.

Size wise, the *Tyrannosaurus rex* had the bigger brain and it is assumed she was more intelligent. Predatory animals are often more intelligent than the herbivores they hunt. Even so, the *Tyrannosaurus rex* is aware of just how dangerous a big, angry male *Triceratops* can be.

This is one meal not worth dying for and she leaves to search for a smaller, young *Triceratops* or even a hadrosaur.

In this evolutionary arms race battle, the *Triceratops* wins.

TYRANNOSAURUS REX

SPEED	7
AVERAGE WEIGHT	6
AGILITY	5
WEAPONS (teeth, horns)	8

The science behind this imaginary encounter is very interesting. The truth is that scientists don't know that the horns of a *Triceratops* were for fighting. If they were, then we would expect to see some "perfect arrangement" but there were lots of numbers, shapes and sizes of horns between the *Triceratops* and its relatives.

TRICERATOPS

SPEED	5
AVERAGE WEIGHT	8
AGILITY	5
WEAPONS (teeth, horns)	8

There may be evidence for an encounter between a *Tyrannosaurus rex* and a *Triceratops*. A *Triceratops* fossil shows signs of tooth marks along the cheekbone and the edge of one of the larger horns above the eye. The horn was also fractured and showed signs of healing. What does this mean? Well, a large predator (and the only suspect can be a *Tyrannosaurus rex*) at some point bit a *Triceratops,* but because there was healing, we know it survived the encounter. We don't know how old the animals were when they met, or even who started the fight.

Even though *Tyrannosaurus rex* was one of the most impressive predators ever, don't be fooled into thinking it always went after the biggest animals for food. Think about lions . . . will they take on a huge adult water buffalo (known for their bad temper), or will they go for the young ones or the sick ones or the old ones? Perhaps *Tyrannosaurus rex* would not have been silly enough to tackle an adult *Triceratops*.

Fossil Finder

Finding fossils is fun. Here are some of the skills needed if you want to find your own fossils. It's important always to make sure you look for fossils legally, responsibly and above all, safely! "Fossil Finder" sections in this series will look at where and when are the best places to find fossils, how to take care of them like a museum collection, and how to clean them.

This "Fossil Finder" is the most important of all and looks at the equipment you will need and how to stay safe.

There are rules when you go out hunting for a _Tyrannosaurus rex_. Some are designed to protect you and some to protect the fossils and the landscape.

 Never go fossil hunting on your own, even if you know the area well.

 Always take an adult with you.

 Many sites that are good for fossils are remote and you could easily get into trouble with rising tides, rocks falling from cliffs or getting stuck in mud.

Take a flashlight and some brightly colored clothes, and bring a phone.

 If you are going anywhere near cliffs, think about taking a hard hat too!

 Check tide timetables if you are going to bays and coves.

 Never search for fossils at the bottom of cliffs. Falling rocks are a danger, so unless you are a paleontologist, don't do it!

 Stay at least 25 ft. away from the base of cliffs.

 Be careful of steep drops and never go fossil hunting in quarries.

 Winter is a good time to look for fossils because heavy rain and storms often reveal them, but make sure you keep warm and wrap up well.

Always think about your safety when looking for fossils.

You will need some equipment to collect properly, get all the information you can and prevent any damage to the fossils on your way home.

 The most important tool for any fossil hunter is a notebook and pencil.

 Record where you found the fossil and when.

 Draw the scene – was it near the sea or in a stream bed? Was it next to other rocks and what did they look like? Writing notes and making detailed sketches will help you remember and make you a better scientist.

 A camera is also a good way of recording lots of information and for you to keep a record of all your finds.

 Take some newspaper to wrap your fossil in and prevent damage.

 A magnifying glass is handy, to make sure you're looking at an actual fossil.

 If you break rocks apart to see if there are fossils inside you'll need a little hammer and chisel and safety glasses too, remember.

It's not just you that needs looking after though . . .
if you go fossil hunting, you need to be a responsible
collector. We'll look at how to collect fossils responsibly
in another "Fossil Finder" section. As long as it is done
safely and in a way that doesn't destroy valuable fossils
for anyone else, hunting for fossils is a perfect way to
practice being a young scientist or naturalist. You'll
learn lots about identifying species and you'll have
some great adventures finding weird and wonderful
specimens. Happy hunting!

Quiz Answers

p 36

Are all the dinosaurs dead?
No.

What does bipedal mean?
Walks on two legs.

How many dinosaur species do we know about?
1,000, with more discoveries all the time.

What three things do most dinos have in common?
See the dino checklist on p 23. Did you get three
of these?

What group does _T. rex_ belong to?
Theropods or Tyrannosaurids.

Name two of _T. rex_'s relatives.
Did you get any two of _Gorgosaurus_, _Daspletosaurus_,
Tarbosaurus or _Albertosaurus_?

p 66

How long is the biggest _T. rex_ tooth found so far?
About 12 in.

Which period did the _T. rex_ live in?
The Cretaceous.

Which period did the first flowering plants evolve in?
The Jurassic.

What is Laramidia?
A continent made up from one long island that existed between 99.6 million and 66 million years ago.

How many vertebrae in a _T. rex_'s tail?
Up to 40.

p 78

The colors in the fossil feather are:
Black, white, red, white and red.

How many did you get?

Glossary

Belemnite A group of extinct cephalopods (which includes animals like octopuses, squid and cuttlefish). They looked like squid and had ten tentacles with little hooks on them. Unlike squid, they had a hard internal skeleton or shell (often found on beaches). They are called belemnite bullets because of their shape.

Biomechanics The study of animals and plants and their "mechanics," looking at things like how they move or support weight and how certain structures, such as the heart, work.

Bipedal Walking on two legs. Humans, birds and theropod dinosaurs are all bipedal.

Carnivore Meat eater.

Cretaceous A geological period in the history of Earth.

Diapsid Means "two arches." This group includes crocodiles, lizards, snakes, turtles and dinosaurs.

Digit A finger or toe.

Ecosystem The network (or community) of species all interacting in one particular environment.

Femur The "thigh" bone, usually the longest bone in the body.

Herbivore Plant eater.

Heterodont When the teeth show differences.

Homodont When the teeth all look the same.

Humerus The longest bone in the top of the upper limb (arm), attaching to the shoulder blade and the radius and ulna.

Jurassic A geological period in the history of Earth.

Laramidia A continent made up from one big, long island. It existed between 99.6 million and 66 million years ago.

Maastrichtian The last stage of the Cretaceous period.

Maxilla Upper jaw.

Melanosomes Tiny structures found in animal cells, responsible for making and storing melanin. Melanin is a type of pigment that helps give color to cells and structures in animals' bodies.

Mesozoic The Mesozoic Era was made up of the Triassic, Jurassic and Cretaceous periods.

Metacarpal The digits on the forelimb (hand). Each digit there starts with a metacarpal and ends in phalanges.

Olfactory Sense of smell.

Omnivore Meat and plant eater.

Paleontologist A scientist who uses fossils to help study and understand more. Paleontologists can study lots of things, including dinosaurs, plants, mammals, insects and fish.

Radius One of the two long bones stretching between the humerus and hand.

Quadrupedal Walking on four legs. Dogs, bears, stegosaurs and *Triceratops* are all quadrupeds.

Sauropod Meaning "lizard-footed."

Synapsid Means "fused arch" and includes mammals and some earlier groups. Synapsids have skulls with a hole behind each eye, which allows strong muscle attachments to the jaw.

Theropod dinosaurs The actual word means "beast foot" and refers to a large group of bipedal dinosaurs. Many were carnivores but there were herbivore and omnivore theropod dinosaurs.

Triassic A geological period in the history of Earth.

Tyrannosaurid Any member of the family Tyrannosauridae.

Tyrannosauridae The superfamily of theropod dinosaurs and its relatives. These dinosaurs were the top predators in the northern hemisphere during the Jurassic and Cretaceous periods.

Ulna One of the two long bones stretching between the humerus and hand. It joins at the "little finger" side and has a distinctive "U" groove at one end.

PICTURE CREDITS

NOTE from **SCOTT HARTMAN**:

T. rex: The one used is based on the "Sue" specimen at the Field Museum, FMNH PR2081. Sue was found in South Dakota, and is still the most complete *T. rex* known, and also one of the largest.

Visit

www.bengarrod.co.uk

for lots more about
dinosaurs.

BEN GARROD

So You Think You Know About...?

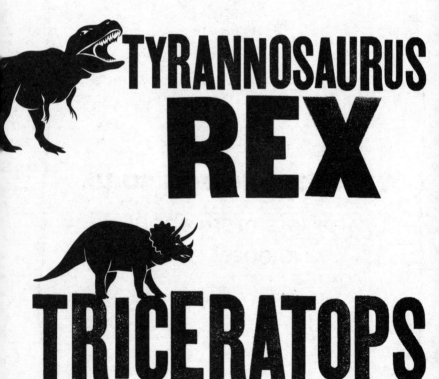

TYRANNOSAURUS REX

TRICERATOPS

VELOCIRAPTOR

STEGOSAURUS

MEET DR. BEN GARROD

Dr. Ben Garrod is an evolutionary biologist, which means he studies how different animals change over time. He has worked worldwide with chimpanzees, whales, sharks and dinosaurs.

As a child growing up by the sea he fell in love with nature. He found his first fossil when he was very small and has loved dinosaurs ever since.

Ben is a TV presenter and a Teaching Fellow at Anglia Ruskin University in the UK.

bengarrod.co.uk

So You Think You Know About...
DINOSAURS?

HAVE YOU GOT THEM ALL?